Get Out of Debt
With Math!

Avoiding, Negotiating, and Paying Down Debt the Smart Way

Tim Hill

Questing Vole Press

Get Out of Debt With Math! Avoiding, Negotiating, and Paying Down Debt the Smart Way
by Tim Hill

Editor: Kevin Debenjak
Proofreader: Diane Yee
Compositor: Kim Frees
Cover: Questing Vole Press

Contents

Introduction

Debt, Today

Debt beyond one's means is as insidious as it is implacable, offering the Faustian bargain of immediate pleasures in exchange for ever-increasing pain. Let's examine and define this problem, and then take the perspective of the ancients, who offer a solution that's been proven to work but has been suppressed by 28 centuries of propaganda.

State-run lotteries are commonly described as "a tax on the mathematically illiterate." Debt is similar but far more burdensome. Buying too many lottery tickets might deprive you of a few coffees and impulse purchases, but debt can cost you your freedom. The media frequently refer to today's "debt slaves" figuratively, but for much of human history debt has led quickly and surely to literal slavery (more on that later).

The reason for this situation is clear to those who know some mathematics. Paying off an interest-bearing loan can require many times the amount of the loan. While the interest accrues relentlessly, without pause, the ability of the debtor to repay almost always varies with any number of variables—the job market, the economy at large, the individual's health. A bit of bad luck, a few missed payments, and compound interest will grind the debtor to dust. This story from an unskilled laborer provides a lesson in how debt works, and why it's so expensive to be poor:

I live with my wife, two children, and my disabled mother in a tiny apartment. I'm barely hanging on—a paycheck away from *destitution. My only luxury is a 60-inch flat-screen TV, which is hanging on my dining-room wall because the living room is Mom's bedroom. I bought the TV from a rent-to-own outlet and I felt pride when I paid it off. Then I got to wondering how much I actually paid for that thing. I kept all the receipts and I added them up. I paid $5200 for that damned TV.*

On every level from personal credit cards to corporate bonds, the debt picture in the world today is grim. Here's a snapshot of U.S. debt at the time of writing:

- **Household debt**, including mortgages, credit cards, auto loans, student loans, and revolving debt, is at an all-time high of $13.5 trillion, and increasing by more than $200 billion per quarter. In a recent three-month period, mortgage debt increased by $141 billion, student debt by $37 billion, auto loans by $27 billion, and credit-card debt by $15 billion—levels not seen since just before the start of the Great Recession, in 2008.

- **Corporate debt**, according to the Forbes magazine article "The U.S. Is Experiencing A Dangerous Corporate Debt Bubble," is in the same disastrous shape as household debt. American corporations owe more money than they ever have, fully 40% more than they owed in 2008, again just before the Great Recession. Corporate managers have been using the money to buy their own companies' shares, to buy other companies, and to otherwise enrich corporate managers and shareholders without actually increasing sales or profits.

- **National debt**—the federal government of the United States is on track to spend, in the current fiscal year, one trillion dollars more than it takes in, leaving the preceding fiscal year's $21 trillion national debt in the dust. As with corporate and personal debt, this is huge, as we have not seen huge before.

The mathematics of compound interest make it self-evident that this kind of debt is unsustainable and is contributing to a global crash.

The business-as-usual types tell us that nothing can be done, but we must keep going, only faster. The human-nature cynics tell us that nothing can be done because, you know, human nature.

But there exists an ancient road not recently traveled, one that successfully dealt with the intractable problem of debt for many thousands of years. It can't save us from the crash that's already in progress, but it's certainly worth knowing about when we start over.

The Cradle of Debt

Western civilization began to flourish about 6000 years ago, not long after agriculture replaced hunting and gathering as the occupation of most humans, on the fertile ground between the Tigris and Euphrates rivers. The region is known in history as Mesopotamia, a cradle of civilization, and is known today as Iraq and Syria, war-ravaged graveyards of civilization.

One of the earliest systems of writing (cuneiform) began here, the wheel was invented here, the Semitic languages—Hebrew and Arabic—arose here, metalworking—the Bronze Age—began here, as did mathematics, astronomy, and codified law. These were smart, creative people who, among many other things, experimented with forms of government: city-states, kingdoms, elements of democracy, and empires.

Thanks to breakthroughs in decoding ancient languages, modern scholars have discovered that, very early on, these shrewd ancients all appear to have recognized the toxicity of debt shortly after its invention. For some time the revelations about debt were particular to some time frame or ruler being studied, but a few scholars began to see and pursue a wider pattern. The foremost among them, Prof. Michael Hudson of the University of Missouri, has spent 30 years unraveling this pattern, with surprising results.

By 4500 years ago, virtually every king, emperor, and warrior priest in all of Mesopotamia had come to understand that an economy based on agriculture can't thrive—or even survive—if the people who do the farming are disaffected. For more than a thousand years they had seen debt run out of control, over and over again, turning hardscrabble farmers into rebels or migrants, to the extreme detriment of their kingdoms and empires.

The leaders realized that the iron nature of debt is to grow out of control until the debtor defaults and the creditor takes ownership of his land, wife, daughters, and his person. The point of early money-lending appears not to be interest earned, but land grabbed and people enslaved—guaranteeing a populace brimming with unhappy, unproductive farmers.

It's not the case, as we might suppose, that these farmers got themselves into trouble by profligate spending. Their economies were based on credit, but not on loans. Their income was the harvest, and it happened once a year, so in the interim the brewer of beer, the baker of bread, and the other providers of necessities kept accounts to be settled with payments of grain made on the threshing floor. They extended credit, not loans, and no interest accrued.

It wasn't irresponsible gambling and drinking debts that made a loan necessary; it was a bad harvest, a sudden tax levy by a greedy king, or some other misfortune that threatened the ability of the farmer to keep his land. In his need he would find all too many lenders able and willing to make him a loan, secured by his land, wife, daughters, and person. All too often, the loan turned out to be his final misfortune.

What the leaders understood (by about 2500 BCE) was that their own survival depended on the welfare of farmers, and that any system that didn't keep the farmers' heads above water would fail. And so they fixed it. In the ancient kingdoms of Sumer, in the empires of Akkadia and Assyria and Babylonia, they cured the scourge of debt. They lifted its yoke from their subjects and because they did, they survived for two thousand years to nurture the civilizations whose descendants today bestride much of the world and embody all the hard-won lessons of life in ancient Mesopotamia.

Except one. What they learned and did about debt has been almost completely expunged from history, and even from the Bible, in what amounts to 28 centuries of fake news.

Debt Amnesty

When the potentates and kings of Bronze Age Mesopotamia realized that interest-bearing debt would inevitably destroy first the lower classes and then the entire kingdom (or empire, or whatever form of government they were using at the time), they reacted forcefully and logically. They canceled all debts, periodically.

Not merely once every 49 years, as the Bible would later recommend, but every once in a while—when a new king took the throne, on an anniversary of the empire, or because it was Friday (the seven-day week was first defined by the Babylonians). Every language used in the region for more than 2000 years has a term for the practice. In his book *...and forgive them their debts: Lending, Foreclosure and Redemption From Bronze Age Finance to the Jubilee Year*, Michael Hudson translates the term as "Clean Slate Amnesty."

A Clean Slate Amnesty proclamation (of which many examples survive—one of which is reproduced in triplicate on the Rosetta Stone) canceled all outstanding interest-bearing loans; freed from bondage all those who had been enslaved because of debt; and restored to the original owner land that had been foreclosed upon. Leaders did this often, at different times, in many kingdoms and empires, whenever debt began destroying the health of their economy. As a result, writes Hudson:

> *By liberating distressed individuals who had fallen into debt bondage, and returning to cultivators the lands they had forfeited for debt or sold under economic duress, these royal acts maintained a free peasantry willing to fight for its land and work on public building projects and canals.... By clearing away the buildup of personal debts, rulers saved society from the social chaos that would have resulted from personal insolvency, debt bondage, and military defection.*

The mere idea of sweeping debt cancellation sets Western civilization rigid with indignation. Failure to pay one's debts is immoral, as we've all been taught for centuries. In fact, it's the very definition of immorality, given that in many languages the word for "debt" and the word for "sin" are the same word. (The seldom-observed Jubilee discussed in the Bible (Leviticus) and in Hebrew tradition doesn't appear to be the same thing as a Clean Slate Amnesty.)

The rulers of Mesopotamia, on the other hand, regarded it as immoral to allow people who preyed upon the least fortunate to destroy not only the poor people but the kingdom. It was immoral to make a loan that the borrower clearly would be unable to repay, so that the lender could foreclose on him and his land and his family. It was immoral to let an ever-widening wedge be driven between the wealthy lenders and the poor borrowers, until the deprived borrowers had nothing left to do but emigrate, revolt, or die.

The wisdom of the Bronze Age in Mesopotamia was to treat debt as a tumor to be removed whenever it grew too big, for the good of the body politic. This point of view and course of action, so utterly at odds with the conventional wisdom of many generations, is now almost inconceivable. The practice was unknown to the foundational philosophers of our time, from Karl Marx to Adam Smith to the founders of the American Republic. This option never occurred to them, and so it never occurs to us, being victims of a successful, centuries-long public-relations campaign by vile and rapacious people. By about 1000 BCE, wealthy lenders had learned how to influence political decision-makers, so that by the time of the rise of the Greek city-states and the Roman Empire, after 800 BCE, Clean Slate Amnesty proclamations became vanishingly rare, interest-bearing loans became more permanent, and loan repayments became sacred obligations not to be forgiven by anybody.

Moneylenders 1, Jesus 0

The rising moneyed classes of the ancient world went to great lengths to eradicate the long-standing tradition of periodic debt amnesties. In fact, the historical record can be used to argue that Jesus Christ's core mission was to restore Clean Slate Amnesties, or Jubilee. In his first sermon, at the age of 15, Jesus said;

> ... the Lord has anointed me; he has sent me to bring good news to the meek, to bind up the brokenhearted, to proclaim liberty to the captives, and to set the spiritual prisoners free; to proclaim the year of God's favor and the day of our God's reckoning.

This proclamation can be interpreted figuratively—God wants everybody to be happy—or literally—God wants all the debts canceled.

Jesus taught his followers to pray, "forgive us our debts." Only centuries later was the translation of the Lord's Prayer changed to the more opaque, "forgive us our trespasses." (Hardly a coincidence.) Forgiving debts was anathema to the Pharisees, and to the newly ascendant moneyed class cuddling up to the Roman Empire, and as Jesus's message gained traction, so did their desire to see him dead. Jesus didn't die for our sins, he died for our debts. The crucifixion of Jesus was his punishment for his economic views—he was a threat to the creditors.

The Old Testament gave Big Money some headaches as well. The commandment against coveting your neighbor's wife, for example, isn't about forbidding adultery but about forbidding the common practice of lending money for the purpose of foreclosing on the borrower's wife. The Bible contains many other stories and approbations that have been edited, truncated, retranslated, or otherwise revised so that they no longer point to debt forgiveness by the upper classes, but to obedience of the lower classes leading to spiritual, not economic, well-being.

The moneylenders ultimately won, although not every battle in every era. The Greek Orthodox Church held on to regular debt cancellation for a few centuries. The Catholic Church in medieval Europe refused the sacraments, and Christian burial, to anyone who charged any interest (usury) on any loan. But such setbacks for the wealthy were brief and few. Now it's firmly established in the communal mind of Western civilization that debts and the rights of creditors are sacred, as is the obligation of debtors to repay every cent borrowed. The larger obligations of the creditors to the system that nurtures them have been expunged from our consciousness. But not from the historical record. The political fight of Jesus and countless debtors has spanned thousands of years and dozens of civilizations. This battle originates from the mathematics of compound interest: collective debt always grows faster than the ability to pay.

The Mathematics of Money

By now you should despise all your past, present, and future creditors. A general debt amnesty isn't out of the question; as we saw in 2008, our teetering monetary system will go to extraordinary and unexpected lengths to save itself. In the meantime, your best weapon is a practical grasp of the mathematics of compound interest, which you can use to understand, avoid, negotiate, renegotiate, and pay down your debts.

The material in this book requires a command of high-school mathematics, especially exponents, logarithms, geometric series, sigma notation, and some statistics. In a few places, the tools of elementary calculus—derivatives, Taylor series, L'Hôpital's rule, and iteration—are used to prove a result, solve an equation, or derive an optimal value. If you like, you can skip or skim the calculus-based parts without loss of continuity. Chapter 10 provides a mathematical refresher and a short list of key mathematical facts.

Keep in mind that mathematical concepts aren't confined to the context in which they're introduced. You can apply the methods in this book to a wide variety of problems. As illustrated by various examples, the same calculations that determine mortgage payments can also help you decide how to pay down credit-card debt, and the optimal strategy for investing in speculative business ventures also applies to casino betting.

1

Interest

When you borrow money for a period of time, **interest** will be charged by the lender (think of interest as the cost of using someone else's money). Conversely, when you lend money you will receive interest. Interest is payment above repayment of the amount borrowed, at a particular rate. This interest is either **simple** or **compound**, and the dramatic difference between the two is best illustrated with an example. Suppose that you invest $100 for 100 years at an annual interest rate of 5%.

- With simple interest, $5 is added each year, or $5 × 100 = $500 in total, so the end total is $100 + $500 = $600.

- With compound interest, let S and E denote the amounts at the start and end of a given year, respectively. During the year, 5% of S is added, so $E = S(1 + 5/100)$. This addition happens every year, so after 100 years the total amount that you have is $100(1 + 5/100)^{100} = $13,150.13.

Note that interest is distinct from any fees that a lender might charge a borrower in addition to interest. Unless otherwise specified, interest calculations in this book

- Use compound interest

- Ignore fees and other transaction costs

- Use natural (base e) logarithms, denoted by $\log(x)$, $\log_e(x)$, or $\ln(x)$

Example 1.1   Suppose that you borrow an amount C on which you're charged an annual rate of interest of r%. If you make no repayments, then how much will you owe after n years?

Solution   After n years, you'll owe

$$C(1 + r/100)^n$$

Example 1.2   If the annual interest rate is 12%, and you borrow $1000 for six months, then how much should you repay?

Solution   It's tempting to think that by borrowing for half a year the interest charge is 6% (half of 12%), so the repayment should be $1060. This answer is incorrect, however. Let x% be the interest rate for six months. After six months you owe $1000(1 + x/100)$, so after another six months, one year in total, you would owe $1000(1 + x/100)^2$. Because the annual rate is 12%, we have

$$1000\left(1 + \frac{x}{100}\right)^2 = 1000\left(1 + \frac{12}{100}\right),$$

leading to

$$1 + \frac{x}{100} = \sqrt{1.12} = 1.0583\ldots.$$

The interest rate for six months is actually 5.83%, so you should repay $1058.30.

Example 1.3   If the annual rate is 12%, and you borrow $1000 for one month, then how much should you repay?

Solution   The appropriate interest rate is that value x such that

$$1000\left(1 + \frac{x}{100}\right)^{12} = 1000\left(1 + \frac{12}{100}\right),$$

giving $1 + x/100 = 1.12^{1/12} \approx 1.0094888$. The interest rate for one month is 0.94888%, so you should repay $1009.49.

Example 1.4   What is the annual interest rate if a bank advertises (a) a quarterly interest rate of 2%, (b) 1% per month?

Solution   (a) After a full year of four quarters, with 2% interest charged each time, a loan of size C becomes $C(1.02)^4 \approx 1.0824C$. The true annual interest rate is 8.24%, not the 8% that the bank suggests.

(b) A rate of 1% per month means that the debt is $C(1.01)^{12} \approx 1.1268C$ at the year's end—a true annual rate of 12.68%, not 12%.

No matter how an interest rate is presented or quoted, you can use a simple two-step process to calculate how much is owed at any specified future time.

1. If necessary, convert the rate to the true annual rate by using the method shown in the preceding example.

2. With r% as the true annual rate, calculate the amount owed when borrowing C for t years (t can be a whole number or a fraction) as

$$C\left(1+\frac{r}{100}\right)^t.$$

We say that interest is **compounded continuously.**

Example 1.5   If the true annual interest rate is 10%, then how much should you repay if you borrow $1000 for (a) six months, (b) 40 months?

Solution   (a) Six months is half a year, so you should repay $1000(1.10)^{1/2} =$ $1048.81.

(b) 40 months is three and one-third years, so you should repay $1000(1.10)^{10/3} =$ $1373.96.

Example 1.6   A loan is offered at 15% interest compounded quarterly. Show that the true annual rate is about 15.865%. Find the true annual rate, to three decimal places, if the nominal rate is 15% compounded (a) monthly, (b) weekly, (c) daily, (d) hourly, (e) more frequently (continuously).

Solution If you borrow an amount C on these terms, then after one year of four quarters you'll owe $C(1 + 0.15/4)^4 = C \cdot 1.158650\ldots$, so the true rate is about 15.865%.

(a) Monthly, $(1 + 0.15/12)^{12} = 1.160754\ldots$, so the rate is 16.075%.

(b) Weekly, $(1 + 0.15/52)^{52} = 1.161583\ldots$, so the rate is 16.158%.

(c) Daily, $(1 + 0.15/365)^{365} = 1.161798\ldots$, so the rate is 16.180%.

(d) Hourly, $(1 + 0.15/8760)^{8760} = 1.161832\ldots$, so the rate is 16.183%.

(e) Continuously, $\exp(0.15) = e^{0.15} = 1.161834\ldots$; the limit is also a rate of 16.183%.

Example 1.7 You invest \$10,000 in property, which increases in value at the compound rate of 5% annually, but you are charged 2% of the total value at the end of each year. What will your investment be worth at the end of five years?

Solution If, at the beginning of any year, your investment is worth C, then it increases to $1.05C$, but the 2% charge then turns this amount into $1.05C \times 0.98 = 1.029C$, so at the end of 5 years, you'll have $1.0295C$, or about \$11,536.57. Note that a 5% increase, with a 2% decrease, is not the same as a 3% increase.

Example 1.8 You borrow an amount C at r% annual interest. If you make no repayments, then at what time will your debt double?

Solution Your debt will double at that time n when

$$C(1 + r/100)^n = 2C;$$

that is, when $n \log(1 + r/100) = \log(2) = 0.69314718\ldots$. Thus

$$n = \frac{0.693\ldots}{\log(1 + x)},$$

where $x = r/100$. When $|x| < 1$, we have the Taylor series $\log(1 + x) = x - x^2/2 + x^3/3 - \cdots$, so when $x \ (> 0)$ is small, the right side of the equation above is *just under* x and consequently n is *just over* $0.693/x = 69.3/r$.

The preceding example justifies a handy method for estimating the doubling time of a debt.

The Rule of 72   At an annual interest rate of $r\%$, it will take approximately $72/r$ years for a debt to double, if no repayments are made.

Naturally, the same argument shows that if you invest a sum of money that earns annual interest of $r\%$, then it will take about $72/r$ years for your investment to double. Also, if inflation is 3% annually, then it will take about 24 years to halve the value of any cash that you hide under your mattress.

We replace 69.3 by the "nearby" number 72 because the latter has many more divisors, often leading to simpler arithmetic. For example, the Rule of 72 indicates that for interest rates of 6% and 12%, it will take about 12 or 6 years respectively for a debt to double. The exact answers are $\log(2)/\log(1.06) = 11.8956\ldots$ years and $\log(2)/\log(1.12) = 6.1162\ldots$ years.

Note that the Rule of 72 gives an answer that's too large when the rate is 6% and too small when the rate is 12%.

Example 1.9   How accurate is the Rule of 72 for interest rates of 4% and of 24%?

Solution   The Rule of 72 gives the time as 18 years for 4% and 3 years for 24%. The exact answers, using $n = \log(2)/\log(1 + x)$ are $17.67\ldots$ years and $3.22\ldots$ years, respectively, so the Rule of 72 yields answers that are about 1.85% too big, and 6.9% too small, in these cases.

The preceding examples illustrate the general result that there's an interest rate ($\approx 7.85\%$) below which the Rule of 72 *overestimates* the doubling time, and above which *underestimates* it.

Here we use the tools of elementary calculus to prove that there exists a unique value x such that the Rule of 72 overestimates the doubling time when $0 < r < x$, and underestimates it when $r > x$, where $r\%$ denotes an interest rate.

Let $E(r) = \log(2)/\log(1 + r/100)$ be the exact doubling time and $R(r) = 72/r$ be the approximate time given by the Rule of 72. To compare $E(r)$ and $R(r)$, it's easier to look at the graphs of their reciprocals

$$F(r) = \log(1 + r/100)/\log(2)$$

and

$$S(r) = r/72.$$

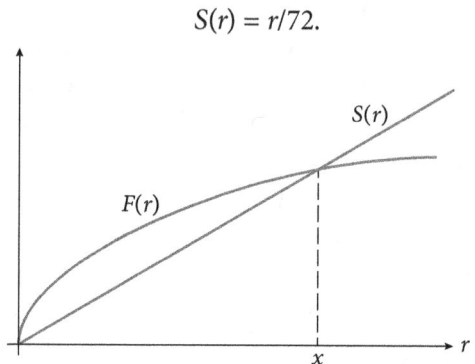

Clearly, $F(0) = S(0) = 0$. Differentiating,

$$S'(r) = 1/72 \quad \text{(a constant)}$$

and

$$F'(r) = \frac{1}{\log(2)} \cdot \frac{1}{(1+r/100)} \cdot \frac{1}{100} = \frac{1}{\log(2) \cdot (100+r)},$$

so $F'(0) = 1/(100 \log(2)) \approx 1/69.3$ exceeds $S'(0) = 1/72$.

The graph of $F(r)$ initially rises more steeply than that of $S(r)$, but its slope decreases monotonically to zero. For small r, $F(r) > S(r)$, meaning that $E(r) < R(r)$; that is, for such values of r, the Rule of 72 *overestimates* the doubling time.

Because F' decreases monotonically and becomes less than $S' = 1/72$, there exists a unique point $x > 0$ where $F(x) = S(x)$ and the Rule of 72 gives the *exact* doubling time. For $r > x$, $F(r) < S(r)$—meaning that $E(r) > R(r)$—and the Rule of 72 *underestimates* the doubling time.

To find the crossover point x, we solve $F(x) = S(x)$ by using Newton-Raphson iteration, with

$$f(x) = x - 72 \log(1 + x/100)/\log(2) = x - K \log(1 + x/100),$$

so that

$$f'(x) = 1 - K/(100 + x),$$

where $K = 72/\log(2) \approx 103.874$. We now have the iteration $x_{n+1} = x_n - f(x_n)/f'(x_n)$. Based on our work so far, we choose 8% as the initial guess of the crossover point, so $x_0 = 8$, $x_1 = 7.85$, $x_2 = 7.847$, $x_3 = 7.8469$. To three significant figures, $x = 7.85$. The changeover point is close to $r = 7.85\%$.

2

Present Value

Would you prefer a gift of $1000 now, or a gift of $10,000 two years from now? Only in unusual or desperate circumstances would you take the immediate money, but what if the alternative is $1100 in two years' time? The choice is no longer obvious. To choose correctly, you must answer the general question: how much is it worth *now* to be offered amount C, but to be received in n years' time?

Suppose that i is the current interest rate. If you had amount X now, then that would become $X(1 + i)^n$ in n years, so setting $C = X(1 + i)^n$ leads to $X = C/(1 + i)^n$. In other words, having $C/(1 + i)^n$ *now* is equivalent to having C in n years time (n can be a whole number or a fraction). We say that the **present value**, or **PV**, of the offer is

$$PV = \frac{C}{(1+i)^n}.$$

This concept lets us make sensible comparisons. In the scenario above, the present value of receiving $1100 two years hence would be equivalent to $1000 now, provided that, with an interest rate of i, $1100/(1 + i)^2 = 1000$; that is, when $i = 4.88\%$. For lower interest rates, the delayed gift is preferred, for higher rates the immediate cash is more attractive. Solving this equation for i is easy to do algebraically, but you can also use the spreadsheet formula =RATE(2,,1000,-1100).

If a stream of money is expected at different future times, then the PV of that stream is the sum of the PVs of each cash flow. For example, a company might invest in an expensive piece of machinery now expecting to generate a stream of higher future profits. The times at which those profits appear, as well as the amounts, are crucial: an extra million dollars tomorrow is worth far more than a million dollars 20 years hence. Formally, if i is the interest rate, and an amount c_k arises at the end of year k for $k = 1, 2, \ldots, n$, then the PV of this income stream is

$$PV = \sum_{k=1}^{n} \frac{c_k}{(1+i)^k}.$$

Major long-term government infrastructure projects—high-speed rail links, highways, bridges, airports, dams—typically run many billions of dollars and have distant completion times. To make sense, economic justifications for such projects must account for *when* costs will be incurred, and benefits seen. Simply assessing and adding the sums involved is of no value.

Example 2.1   What (sensible) interest rates make receiving $1000 now preferable to $2000 in one year's time, then repaying $910 one year later?

Solution   Let i denote the interest rate. Repaying an amount means receiving the *negative* of that amount, so the present value of the second offer is

$$\frac{2000}{1+i} - \frac{910}{(1+i)^2}.$$

The immediate gift is preferable if

$$1000 > \frac{2000}{1+i} - \frac{910}{(1+i)^2}.$$

Let $x = 1 + i$ and simplify the preceding equation as

$$100x^2 - 200x + 91 > 0.$$

Factoring this quadratic equation, we get

$$(10x - 13)(10x - 7) > 0.$$

The roots are $x = 13/10$ and $x = 7/10$, corresponding to interest rates of $i = 0.3$ and $i = -0.3$. The quadratic is positive when $i > 0.3$ (and when $i < -0.3$).

Hence if $i > 0.3$—that is, interest rates exceed 30%—then the PV of the immediate $1000 is higher, whereas for (positive) interest rates below 30%, the delayed offer with repayment has a higher PV.

Example 2.2 Three alternative income streams are listed below. The stream values are the amounts (in $1000s) that will be paid to you at the ends of years 1, 2, 3, 4, and 5.

A: 12, 14, 16, 18, 20 (total 80)
B: 16, 16, 15, 15, 15 (total 77)
C: 20, 16, 14, 12, 10 (total 72)

Consider possible interest rates of 10%, 20%, and 30%. Find the present values of each income stream and decide, for each interest rate, which stream has the largest present value.

Solution For stream A at 10%, the present value is

$$\frac{12}{1.1} + \frac{14}{1.1^2} + \frac{16}{1.1^3} + \frac{18}{1.1^4} + \frac{20}{1.1^5} = 59.21.$$

Similar calculations yield:

$r = 10\%$: A = 59.21, B = 58.60, C = 56.33. A is best.
$r = 20\%$: A = 45.70, B = 46.39, C = 45.69. B is best.
$r = 30\%$: A = 36.49, B = 37.89, C = 38.12. C is best.

Example 2.3 You borrow $100 from a friend, which you'll repay with two equal payments of $70 at the end of years one and two. Use the concept of present value to determine the interest rate of this loan.

Solution If the interest rate is i, then equating present values gives

$$100 = 70/(1 + i) + 70/(1 + i)^2.$$

Let $x = 1/(1 + i)$, so that $70x^2 + 70x - 100 = 0$, or $7x^2 + 7x - 10 = 0$. Thus

$$x = \frac{-7 \pm \sqrt{49 + 280}}{14}.$$

Taking the positive root, we have $x = 0.795596939\ldots$, leading to $i = 0.2569178\ldots$. The annual interest rate is about 25.7%.

Example 2.4   Shares in XYZ Corp. will pay annual dividends. The initial dividend amount is D, paid one year after purchase. This amount will increase at the compound rate r each year. Let i ($> r$) be the interest rate used to compute present values. Show that the present value of the total of all the dividends that will ever be paid into the indefinite future is $D/(i - r)$.

Solution   The amount to be paid in dividends in n years' time will be $D(1 + r)^{n-1}$, so its present value is $D(1 + r)^{n-1}/(1 + i)^n = Du^{n-1}/(1 + i)$, where $u = (1 + r)/(1 + i)$. Hence the present value of the total amount of all future dividends is

$$\sum_{n=1}^{\infty} \frac{Du^{n-1}}{1+i} = \frac{D}{(1-u)(1+i)}.$$

Substituting, we get $1 - u = 1 - (1 + r)/(1 + i) = (i - r)/(1 + i)$, so the present value is indeed $D/(i - r)$.

3

Annual
Percentage Rate

$\mathcal{S}$uppose that Bank 1 offers you a loan of size L, to be repaid via installments of sizes S_1, S_2, S_3,... at respective times $t_1 < t_2 < t_3 < \cdots$. Additionally, Bank 2 offers you the same amount L, but with a different repayment schedule. To compare such offers, you can calculate their **annual percentage rate**, or **APR**, which is defined to be that interest rate i that makes the present value of the repayments equal to the amount loaned.

To find the APR, we calculate how much is still owed after each repayment. After repaying S_1 at time t_1, you owe

$$L(1+i)^{t_1} - S_1.$$

At time $t_2 - t_1$ later, you pay S_2, hence you now owe

$$(L(1+i)^{t_1} - S_1)(1+i)^{t_2-t_1} - S_2 = L(1+i)^{t_2} - S_1(1+i)^{t_2-t_1} - S_2.$$

Continuing in this way, we see that the amount remaining after the nth repayment reduces to

$$L(1+i)^{t_n} - S_1(1+i)^{t_n-t_1} - S_2(1+i)^{t_n-t_2} - \cdots - S_n.$$

Equate this expression to zero to mark the final repayment, then divide through by $(1+i)^{t_n}$ to get the equation

$$L = \sum_k \frac{S_k}{(1+i)^{t_k}}.$$

Solve this equation to find i, the APR. The APR is meant to reflect the true cost of a loan, taking into account any fees, the frequency and amounts of repayments, all calculated in the same "fair" way.

Example 3.1 You want to borrow $5000. Bank X offers a repayment schedule of $1500 every year for five years. Bank Y offers a repayment schedule of $1000 every year for nine years. Repayments begin one year after the loan is disbursed. Which APR is lower?

Solution For Bank X, we must solve

$$5000 = 1500 \sum_{k=1}^{5} \left(\frac{1}{1+i} \right)^k$$

for i. Let $x = 1/(1 + i)$ and expand the equation to get

$$5000/1500 = 10/3 = x + x^2 + \cdots + x^5.$$

To solve this equation, we recognize that it has the form $A = x + x^2 + \cdots + x^K$; that is, $A = x(1 - x^K)/(1 - x)$, and so can be converted to $x = g(x)$ form as

$$x = \frac{A + x^{K+1}}{A+1}.$$

We use the fixed-point iteration $x_{n+1} = g(x_n)$ with the initial guess $x_0 = 0.9$ to find x, and hence i. The APR is 15.24%.

A similar argument for the terms offered by Bank Y leads to

$$5000/1000 = 5 = x + x^2 + \cdots + x^9,$$

with an APR of 13.70%.

Although you would repay $9000 to Bank Y, but only $7500 to Bank X, Bank Y offers a lower APR.

Example 3.2 A loan of $1000 now is to be paid off by five equal annual installments of $250, starting one year from now. What is the APR (to three significant figures)?

Solution We must solve

$$1000 = \sum_{k=1}^{5} \frac{250}{(1+i)^k}$$

for i. Let $x = 1/(1 + i)$ and expand the equation to get

$$1000/250 = 4 = (x + x^2 + \cdots + x^5).$$

As in Example 3.1, we use the fixed-point iteration $x_{n+1} = g(x_n)$ where $g(x) = 1 - x(1 - x^5)/4$. Let $x_0 = 0.9$ be the initial guess to find x, and hence i. The result converges to $x = 0.926518\ldots$, so the APR ($= i$) is 7.93% to three significant figures.

Example 3.3 You borrow $100 from a payday loan company that charges 0.8% per day *simple* interest. How much will you pay back if you clear your debt after (a) 8 days, (b) 13 days, (c) 20 days? What are the respective APRs?

Solution (a) The total simple interest charge is $0.80 × 8 = $6.40, so you must pay $106.40 to clear the debt. If the APR is r, then we must solve

$$100\left(1 + \frac{r}{100}\right)^t = 106.40,$$

where $t = 8/365$ is the fraction of a year for which you borrowed the money. Thus

$$\frac{8}{365}\log\left(1 + \frac{r}{100}\right) = \log\left(\frac{106.40}{100}\right) = \log(1.064) = 0.062035;$$

that is, $\log(1 + r/100) = 2.83036$, so $r/100 = 15.95$. Hence the APR is about 1595%.

(b) The total simple interest charge is $0.80 × 13 = $10.40, so you must pay $110.40 to clear the debt. If the APR is r, then we must solve

$$100\left(1 + \frac{r}{100}\right)^t = 110.40,$$

where $t = 13/365$ is the fraction of a year for which you borrowed the money. Thus

$$\frac{13}{365}\log\left(1 + \frac{r}{100}\right) = \log\left(\frac{110.40}{100}\right) = \log(1.104) = 0.09894;$$

that is, $\log(1 + r/100) = 2.7779$, so $r/100 = 15.09$. Hence the APR is about 1509%.

(c) The total simple interest charge is $0.80 × 20 = $16.00, so you must pay $116 to clear the debt. If the APR is r, then we must solve

$$100\left(1+\frac{r}{100}\right)^t = 116.00,$$

where $t = 20/365$ is the fraction of a year for which you borrowed the money. Thus

$$\frac{20}{365}\log\left(1+\frac{r}{100}\right) = \log\left(\frac{116.00}{100}\right) = \log(1.16) = 0.14842;$$

that is, $\log(1 + r/100) = 2.708665$, so $r/100 = 14.01$. Hence the APR is about 1401%.

---

4   Mortgages

The largest financial commitment that many people make is to borrow money to buy a house. If you borrow an amount C, at annual interest rate $i > 0$, paying off the same amount each month for n years, then how much will you pay?

Consider one month at a time: let C_k be the amount owed at the end of month k, so that $C_0 = C$, and suppose that R is repaid each month, starting one month after you receive the loan. With an annual interest rate of i, suppose that the corresponding *monthly* rate is r, found by solving $1 + i = (1 + r)^{12}$. At the end of month one, the amount owed is

$$C_1 = C(1 + r) - R.$$

Similarly, the amount owed at the end of month two is

$$C_2 = C_1(1 + r) - R.$$

Using the first equation to replace C_1, we get

$$C_2 = C(1 + r)^2 - R(1 + r) - R.$$

Then, from

$$C_3 = C_2(1 + r) - R,$$

we get

$$C_3 = C(1 + r)^3 - R(1 + r)^2 - R(1 + r) - R,$$

which leads to the general relation

$$C_k = C(1+r)^k - R\sum_{j=0}^{k-1}(1+r)^j \qquad (4.1).$$

There are $m = 12n$ months in n years, so repaying the entire amount after m months means that $C_m = 0$. Hence we find R from the equation

$$0 = C(1+r)^m - R\sum_{j=0}^{m-1}(1+r)^j.$$

The sum is a geometric series. So when $x \neq 1$,

$$\sum_{j=0}^{m-1}x^j = \frac{x^m - 1}{x - 1},$$

and, after some manipulation, because $r > 0$,

$$R = \frac{Cr(1+r)^m}{(1+r)^m - 1} \qquad (4.2)$$

is the monthly repayment. Because we found r via $1 + i = (1 + r)^{12}$, equation (4.2) can also be written as

$$R = \frac{Cr(1+i)^n}{(1+i)^n - 1}.$$

Example 4.1 You borrow $100,000 at 6% annual interest to be repaid over 25 years. (a) How much must you repay each month? (b) How much do you still owe after 15 years? (c) Is it surprising that, after 15 years, you still owe more than half of what you borrowed, despite having made 60% of the payments due?

Solution (a) We have $C = 100,000$, $i = 0.06$, and $n = 25$, so $1.06 = (1 + r)^{12}$, hence $r = 0.4867\%$. From equation (4.2), $R = 634.62$—you pay about $635 every month.

(b) After 15 years (180 months), equation (4.1) shows that the amount still owed is

$$C_{180} = C(1+r)^{180} - R\sum_{j=0}^{179}(1+r)^j$$

$$= C(1+r)^{180} - \frac{R((1+r)^{180} - 1)}{r}.$$

Arithmetic gives an answer of 57,575.55. You still owe $57,575.55.

(c) Each payment must pay off the interest accumulated since the last payment, and also reduce the principal. In the early years of the loan, when the amount owed is greatest, the interest component is considerably higher, so less goes toward reducing the principal still owed.

Example 4.2 A mobile phone costs $200. If you use the store credit card to purchase it, with an annual interest rate of 30%, then the store will reduce the price by 10% to $180. You must pay off this loan over n months, paying equal installments at the end of each month. In total cash terms, compare (a) paying the full price up front in cash and (b) using the store credit card and paying off the loan over 8, 12, or 24 months.

Solution Let R_m be the monthly repayment if you take the credit card loan of $180 for m months. An annual rate of 30% leads to a monthly rate of x%, where $(1 + x/100)^{12} = 1.30$, so the monthly rate is $r = 2.21\%$. Equation (4.2) shows that

$$R_m = \frac{180 \times 0.0221 \times 1.0221^m}{1.0221^m - 1},$$

and the total repaid is $m \cdot R_m$. Over $m = 8$ months, monthly repayments are $R_8 = \$24.79$, so the total repaid is $198.32. Similarly, $R_{12} = \$17.24$ and the total repaid is $206.88, and $R_{24} = \$9.74$ and the total repaid is $233.76. Using the store credit card to get the discount is cheaper than paying cash if you repay over 8 equal monthly installments, but the full cash payment is less than the credit-card cost if you repay over 12 or 24 months.

Example 4.3 To buy a house, you borrow $100,000, to be repaid in equal monthly installments for the next 25 years.

(a) Find the repayments at annual interest rates of (i) 5% and (ii) 10%.

(b) In total, how much more does case (ii) cost than case (i)?

(c) In each case, how much do you owe after 10 years of repayments?

(d) Sketch a graph showing the amount owed against time when the interest rate is 10%.

Solution (a) First, find the monthly interest rate for each case. For an annual rate of 5%, we have $1.05^{1/12} = 1.004074$, so the monthly rate is $r = 0.4074\%$. For an annual rate of 10%, we have $1.10^{1/12} = 1.007974$, so the monthly rate is $r = 0.7974\%$. Next, use equation (4.2) for these values of r, with $C = 100{,}000$ and $m = 300$ months. The respective repayments (rounded) are (i) $R = \$578.13$ and (ii) $R = \$878.48$.

(b) Case (ii) costs $300.35 per month more than case (i), a total of $90,105 over the 25 years (300 months).

(c) After ten years (120 months), the amount remaining is

$$C(1+r)^{120} - R\sum_{k=0}^{119}(1+r)^k.$$

Rewrite this expression as $C(1 + r)^{120} - R((1 + r)^{120} - 1)/r$. At an annual rate of 5%, with $r = 0.004074$ and $R = \$578.13$, you still owe \$73,645.79. At an annual rate of 10%, with $r = 0.007974$ and $R = \$878.48$, you still owe \$83,795.19.

(d)

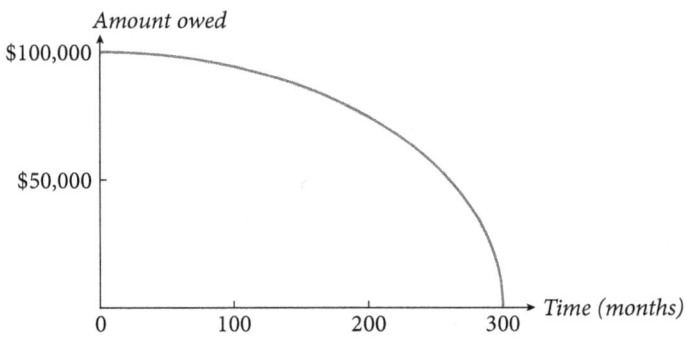

Amount owed

$100,000

$50,000

0   100   200   300   Time (months)

Example 4.4 You take out a mortgage of size $C > 0$, which you'll repay in monthly installments of fixed size R. The *monthly* interest rate is $r > 0$, the first repayment is made one month after the loan is disbursed, and the loan will be repaid fully after N months.

Let $R = KCr$ for some $K > 1$. Deduce that

$$N = \frac{\log(K/(K-1))}{\log(1+r)},$$

and use this result to show that, when r is small, and you make fixed monthly repayments of size $2Cr$, you will repay approximately $1.4C$ altogether, over the lifetime of the mortgage.

Solution   Because $R = KCr$, we have $KCr = C \cdot r \cdot (1 + r)^N/((1 + r)^N - 1)$, so $K((1 + r)^N - 1) = (1 + r)^N$; that is, $(1 + r)^N(K - 1) = K$, from which the given formula follows immediately—divide by $(K - 1)$ and then take logs.

When r is small, $\log(1 + r) \approx r$, and with $K = 2$ you will repay $NR \approx 2C \cdot \log(2)$. But $2 \cdot \log(2) \approx 1.4$, hence the result.

Example 4.5   Your credit card company charges interest monthly, at the annual rate of 25%, on any outstanding debt after the monthly repayment. The rules for this monthly repayment state that any sum of up to $5 must be paid off in full; otherwise, you must pay at least $5, or all the outstanding interest plus 1% of the balance, whichever is greater. Making the minimum repayment, how long would it take you to reduce a debt of $5000 to at most $100?

Solution   The monthly interest is r, where $(1 + r)^{12} = 1.25$; that is, $r = 0.018769\ldots$, so the interest to be paid off when you owe X is rX, and you must also pay $X/100$ against the principal, provided that the sum of these components exceeds 5. If the sum is 5 or below, then you must pay off at least 5. Let D_n be your debt at the end of month n, after you have made your payment. So $D_0 = 5000$ and, initially at least, $D_{n+1} = 0.99D_n$. Because r is almost 2%, effectively you begin by paying some 3% of the balance each month, while the debt reduces by 1%; so until the debt is low enough, you reduce it by only 1% a month. (You can create an spreadsheet to convince yourself.)

The $5 minimum kicks in when $D(r + 0.01) \leq 5$; that is, when $D \leq 174$. Until then, after n months, your debt is 5000×0.99^n, so hitting that level will take 335 months, and you will owe $K_0 = 172.25$ (or so). You now pay 5 each month, part of it interest. Let K_n be what you owe after n months of this payment regime:

$$K_{n+1} = K_n \times (1 + r) - 5,$$

so

$$K_n = K_0(1+r)^n - 5\frac{(1-r)^n - 1}{r}.$$

Thus $K_n \leq 100$ if and only if $(1 + r)^n(K_0 r - 5) \leq 100r - 5$. Solving, we get $n \geq 30.6$, so you pay the minimum for another 31 months. It will take 366 months, more than thirty years, to reduce your debt to $\leq \$100$.

---

5   Annuities

Many people use an **annuity** to provide an income for their retirement. When you take out an annuity, you give money to an insurance company in exchange for a commitment that you will receive a fixed amount monthly for the rest of your life. Exactly the same mathematics that's used to calculate mortgage repayments also applies here because receiving an annuity is the mirror image of paying off a mortgage. Recall equation (4.1):

$$C_k = C(1+r)^k - R\sum_{j=0}^{k-1}(1+r)^j \qquad (4.1).$$

C is now the amount (capital) that you give to the insurance company, i is the annual interest that the company expects to earn from its investments (over and above its own costs), and n is the number of years that they expect to make payments to you, based on your age and health. With r again the monthly interest rate corresponding to i (where $1 + i = (1 + r)^{12}$), equation (4.1) for C_k now represents the amount remaining invested next month. With $m = 12n$, setting C_m equal to zero means that, on average, the insurance company expects to return the capital it received.

Some annuitants will live longer than average, whereas others will die earlier. The insurance company relies on having a large number of customers so that their actuarial estimate of the average lifespan is accurate. The residue from those who die early will let the company meet the payments to unusually long-lived people.

Example 5.1 On your retirement, you have a lump sum of $200,000 to provide an income until you die.

(a) An insurance company estimates that you will live for 20 more years, and assumes it can earn 4% (after its expenses) on the capital you give it. What (fixed) amount would you expect to receive each year?

(b) You believe that you can earn 5% yourself through your skilled investing. Suppose that you're correct, and that you withdraw a fixed income of $20,000 at the end of each year. How long will your fund last?

Solution (a) For the insurance company payment, use equation (4.2) with $r = 4\%$ and $m = 20$. You would expect

$$\$200{,}000 \times 0.04 \times 1.04^{20}/(1.04^{20} - 1) = \$14{,}716.35$$

each year.

(b) In your own hands, let C_k be your capital at the end of year k. Then, as long as your plan lasts, you have $C_{k+1} = 1.05C_k - S$, where S is the income that you withdraw. Thus

$$C_k = 1.05^k C_0 - S(1 + 1.05 + \cdots + 1.05^{k-1}) = 1.05^k C_0 - S\frac{1.05^k - 1}{1.05 - 1}.$$

With $C_0 = 200{,}000$ and $S = 20{,}000$, and as long as $C_k > 0$, this equation reduces to $C_k = 200{,}000(2 - 1.05^k)$. So we need $1.05^k < 2$. Because $1.05^{14} = 1.9799\ldots$ and $1.05^{15} = 2.0789\ldots$, you can live this lifestyle for about 14 years. At the beginning of year 15, your fund has diminished to $C_{14} = \$4013.68$.

Example 5.2 Luke, age 65, will use his savings to buy an annuity. If he buys one now and continues to work, then his salary is large enough that the annuity will be taxed at 40%; but if he postpones buying it until he stops work in five years time, then it will be taxed at only 20%. Postponing buying the annuity also means that the amount it pays will increase by some factor $K > 0$. If his only consideration is financial, how should Luke decide between these alternatives?

Solution One sensible approach is to compare the present values of the alternatives. Assume that Luke's future lifespan is $n > 5$ years. Let

A = annual amount from the annuity (assumed paid at the beginning of a year), and let i be the interest rate used to calculate present values. We calculate the PVs of what Luke receives, after tax.

The PV of the annuity if he buys it immediately is

$$\sum_{r=1}^{5} \frac{(0.6)A}{(1+i)^{r-1}} + \sum_{r=6}^{n} \frac{(0.8)A}{(1+i)^{r-1}}.$$

Postponing purchase for five years, the PV is

$$\sum_{r=6}^{n} \frac{(0.8)A(1+K)}{(1+i)^{r-1}}.$$

Thus buying now is better than postponing if and only if the first expression exceeds the second. Simplifying, we get

$$3\sum_{r=1}^{5} \frac{1}{(1+i)^{r-1}} > 4K\sum_{r=6}^{n} \frac{1}{(1+i)^{r-1}}.$$

Let $x = 1/(1+i) < 1$. We're summing geometric series, so the condition reduces to

$$3(1 - x^5) > 4Kx^5(1 - x^{n-5}).$$

As expected, the values of n for which this condition holds true depend on x and K.

Suppose that $K = 35\%$ (based on common annuity rates of 5.8% at age 65 and 6.8% at age 70, and assuming that Luke's savings fund increases at 3% annually over the five years if he postpones buying the annuity). Also, let $i = 4\%$, so that $x = 1/1.04$. With these values, the criterion becomes $0.5342 > 1.1507(1 - x^{n-5})$, or, using logs, $n < 20.9$. Thus Luke should buy the annuity immediately if he expects to die within about 21 years, but if he expects to live longer, then he should postpone for five years.

If $i = 2\%$, however, then the cutoff is about 18 years; if $i = 6\%$, then the cutoff is about 27 years. How Luke values prospective income in the far future affects the decision he makes now. And other assumptions about K, as well as changes in tax rates, can also lead to different conclusions.

Example 5.3 Alice, age 60, expects to retire in ten years, and has a savings fund to use to buy an annuity at some time. While she works, her annuity income would be taxed at 40%; in retirement, it would be taxed at only 20%. An annuity would pay 5.1% of her savings at age 60, or 6.8% at age 70. If Alice postpones, then she estimates that her savings will increase at 4% annually until she buys the annuity.

How long would Alice need to live to justify postponing for 10 years? Use the present value of the total sum, after tax, that she would receive from her annuity as the criterion. Assume that Alice receives the annual payments at the beginning of each year, and use an interest rate of 5% to calculate present values.

Solution   Assume that Alice's future lifespan is $n > 10$ years. Let $P =$ her savings now. The interest rate used to calculate present values is 5%, so let $x = 1/1.05$. Thus if Alice gets amount A in year r, then its present value is Ax^{r-1}.

If she buys the annuity now, then the PV of the total that she receives is

$$0.051P\left(0.6\sum_{r=1}^{10}x^{r-1} + 0.8\sum_{r=11}^{n}x^{r-1}\right).$$

If she postpones purchase for ten years, then the corresponding PV is

$$0.068P(1.04)^{10}\times0.8\sum_{r=11}^{n}x^{r-1}.$$

For postponing to give a higher PV, we need

$$0.0544\times1.04^{10}\times x^{10}\frac{1-x^{n-10}}{1-x} >$$
$$0.0306\frac{1-x^{10}}{1-x}+0.0408x^{10}\frac{1-x^{n-10}}{1-x}.$$

Rearranging this inequality leads to $0.039725x^n < 0.070325x^{10} - 0.0306 = 0.01257$; that is, $x^n < 0.3165$, or $n > 23.58$ years. Alice needs to live to about 84 for postponing to give a higher PV.

To compensate for inflation, you might want your annual annuity income to rise steadily. The following derivation shows the adjustment that's necessary to recalculate the new payments.

We've seen that the formula for calculating fixed annuity payments is the same as that used for fixed mortgage repayments. Suppose that the insurance company will earn interest at rate $\gamma > 0$ per year, whereas you want the annuity to increase at rate $\beta > 0$ per year. We can adapt the argument leading to equation (4.2) to cover this case, finding the amount of the (initial) annual annuity payment to you, assuming $\gamma \neq \beta$. By fixing γ, and letting β approach γ, we can use L'Hôpital's Rule to find the initial annuity amount when $\gamma = \beta$.

Let R be the initial annuity amount, and C_n be the sum the insurance company has left at the end of year n. Then

$$C_0 = C,$$

$$C_1 = C_0(1 + \gamma) - R,$$

$$C_2 = C_1(1 + \gamma) - R(1 + \beta),$$

and, for $N \geq 3$,

$$C_N = C_{N-1}(1 + \gamma) - R(1 + \beta)^{N-1},$$

giving

$$C_N = C(1+\gamma)^N - R\sum_{k=0}^{N-1}(1+\gamma)^k(1+\beta)^{N-1-k}.$$

Summing the geometric series and setting $C_N = 0$, we see that

$$C(1+\gamma)^N = \frac{R((1+\gamma)^N - (1+\beta)^N)}{\gamma - \beta},$$

where $\gamma - \beta \neq 0$. So the initial annuity amount is

$$R = \frac{C(\gamma - \beta)(1+\gamma)^N}{(1+\gamma)^N - (1+\beta)^N} = \frac{K(\gamma - \beta)}{(1+\gamma)^N - (1+\beta)^N},$$

where $K = C(1 + \gamma)^N$.

To find the limit, let $f(\beta) = K(\gamma - \beta)$ and $g(\beta) = (1 + \gamma)^N - (1 + \beta)^N$, so that $f'(\beta) = -K$, and $g'(\beta) = -N(1 + \beta)^{N-1}$. Thus L'Hôpital's rule means that, as β approaches γ, so R approaches $f'(\gamma) / g'(\beta)$; that is,

$$\frac{K}{N(1+\gamma)^{N-1}} = \frac{C(1+\gamma)}{N},$$

the initial amount when $\gamma = \beta$.

6

Stocks

Conventional wisdom holds that shares of stock, although riskier, tends to produce a higher return than do bank deposits in the long term. The price of shares fluctuates according to what the market thinks they're worth at any time. Suppose that you want to either

(a) pay a fixed amount of money for shares at periodic intervals, or

(b) buy a fixed number of shares at periodic intervals or invest as a lump sum.

Which strategy acquires more shares? Or does it make no difference?

Strategy (a) is often more sensible and is called **dollar-cost averaging**. Depending on the transaction currency, this concept is also called pound-cost averaging, yen-cost averaging, and so on, or, generically, unit-cost averaging. The argument is that when the price of a stock is low you buy more shares and when it's high you buy fewer shares, letting you ride out price fluctuations. In other words, the extra shares that you get when the price is low more than makes up for the fewer you get when the price is high. The more that the share price fluctuates, the greater the advantage of drip-feeding your cash over time.

Let's compare these two strategies over time. Let p_t (> 0) be the share price at time t. In dollar-cost averaging, you invest s dollars at periodic intervals (say, each month), so the number of shares that you would buy each month is

$$n_t = \frac{s}{p_t}.$$

Over a time period T you will have bought

$$\sum_t \frac{s}{p_t} = sT \cdot \frac{1}{T} \sum_t \frac{1}{p_t}$$

shares, which can be rewritten as

$$sT \cdot E\left[\frac{1}{p_t}\right],$$

where E is the expected value (average) operator. Because you've invested sT dollars, you've paid

$$h_t = \frac{1}{E\left[\dfrac{1}{p_t}\right]}$$

per share on average, which is the harmonic mean.

If on the other hand you buy a fixed number of shares n each month, then you would pay np_t each month. Over the time period T you will have paid

$$\sum_t np_t$$

to buy nT shares. Thus you've paid

$$a_t = E[p_t]$$

per share on average, which is the arithmetic mean.

To compare the arithmetic mean a_t to the harmonic mean h_t, we use Jensen's inequality, which states that if $f(x)$ is a convex function, then

$$E[f(x)] \geq f(E[x]).$$

A convex function is a function where a straight line joining any two points on the function (that is, a secant line) lies *above* the graph of the function (well-known examples of convex functions include the x^2 and e^x). Because $1/x$ is a convex function, we have

$$E[1/p_t] \geq 1/E[p_t],$$

which can be rearranged to show that

$$a_t \geq h_t.$$

Thus dollar-cost averaging is always better than or as good as buying the same number of shares each month. To summarize, however the share price fluctuates, we expect at least as many shares if we make n regular purchases, rather than by investing all at once at the average price.

Example 6.1 The prices (in dollars) of shares in XYZ Corp. on the first trading day of the month from January 2018 to December 2018 were 3.02, 2.84, 2.58, 2.29, 1.86, 1.73, 1.85, 1.89, 2.27, 2.44, 2.40, 2.18. How many shares would you have if you invested $12,000 (a) by spending $1,000 on the first trading day of each month; (b) by spending the entire amount at the beginning of the trading period; (c) by spending the entire amount at the average price over the year? (Ignore transaction costs.)

Solution (a) Let p_t be the share price (in dollars) in month t. We calculate

$$\sum_{t=1}^{12} \frac{1000}{p_t},$$

or 5418.6 shares.

(b) The answer is simply 12,000/3.02 = 3973.5 shares.

(c) Using the notation of part (a), the average price is

$$\sum_{t=1}^{12} \frac{p_t}{12} = 2.279,$$

so we would have 12,000/2.279 = 5265.1 shares.

So dollar-cost averaging, as compared to a single purchase at the annual average price, gives 5418.6 − 5265.1 = 155.5 more shares, an increase of 155.5/5265.1 ≈ 3%.

Example 6.2   Over twelve consecutive months, the prices (in dollars) of shares in the ABC mutual fund were 2.49, 2.34, 2.68, 2.75, 2.51, 2.59, 2.37, 2.32, 2.22, 1.75, 1.69, 2.01. The average price is 27.72/12 = 2.31.

(a) If you had $12,000 to spend, how many shares would you have if you paid the average price for every share? How many shares would you have if you spent $1,000 each month, paying that month's price?

(b) If, in the six months where the price was below $2.35, the prices had been $0.30 lower, whereas in the other six months, they had been $0.30 higher, then what would the new figures be for the calculations in part (a)?

(c) Comment on how the advantage of dollar-cost averaging appears to change with the *variability* of the share price.

Solution   (a) At the average price, you would have 12,000/2.31 = 5194.8 shares. With monthly purchases, you would have 1000/2.49 + · · · + 1000/2.01 = 5314.2 shares.

(b) The average is the same (5194.8 shares). The dollar-cost averaging amount is now 5598.4 shares (5.35% higher).

(c) In the second case, where the price is *more* variable, the advantage of dollar-cost averaging is *higher*.

7

Personal Savings

It's sensible to build up savings during your working life. So it's worth making calculations, however speculative, about how much you must save to amass an adequate sum. At its simplest, if you invest X at the beginning of each year for n years, and the annual growth rate is $G > 0$, then the mathematics is similar to that used for mortgage repayments.

Let Y_k be the amount that you'll have at the end of year k. If you invest at the beginning of the year, then you have

$$Y_0 = 0,$$

$$Y_1 = X(1 + G),$$

$$Y_2 = Y_1(1 + G) + X(1 + G) = X(1 + G)^2 + X(1 + G),$$

and so on, giving

$$Y_n = X \sum_{j=1}^{n} (1+G)^j = \frac{X(1+G)((1+G)^n - 1)}{G}.$$

Example 7.1 Alice and Becky are twins. Alice invests X each year for 40 years. Becky starts 20 years later and invests W each year for only 20 years. If both sisters enjoy the same growth rate, then how much more must Becky save to achieve the same final amount as Alice?

Solution For Becky to do as well as Alice, she requires that

$$\frac{X(1+G)((1+G)^{40} - 1)}{G} = \frac{W(1+G)((1+G)^{20} - 1)}{G};$$

that is, $W = X((1 + G)^{20} + 1)$. At a modest growth rate of $G = 3\%$, Becky must save almost three times as much as Alice every year, and if the growth rate is 6%, then she must save 4.2 times as much. The power of compound interest demonstrates the benefits of saving from a young age.

In general, saving X every year for n years will give the same total as saving W every year for m years whenever

$$\frac{X(1+G)((1+G)^n - 1)}{G} = \frac{W(1+G)((1+G)^m - 1)}{G},$$

or

$$\frac{W}{X} = \frac{(1+G)^n - 1}{(1+G)^m - 1}.$$

Let's assess how the growth rate G affects the value of this ratio for general values of m and n. The simplest case should be when $G = 0$, but letting $G = 0$ in this formula results in the nonsensical expression $0/0$. Here, we need L'Hôpital's Rule, which states that if we have some point c where $f(c) = g(c) = 0$, then, provided that all expressions make sense, the limit of $f(G)/g(G)$ is $f'(c)/g'(c)$ as $G \to c$. Here, let

$$f(G) = (1 + G)^n - 1,$$

$$g(G) = (1 + G)^m - 1, \text{ and}$$

$$c = 0.$$

Differentiating, we get

$$f'(G) = n(1 + G)^{n-1}, \text{ and}$$

$$g'(G) = m(1 + G)^{m-1},$$

so their ratio $f'(G)/g'(G)$ reduces to

$$(n/m)(1 + G)^{n-m}.$$

L'Hôpital's Rule tells us that, as $G \to 0$, the ratio W/X tends to n/m. This result makes sense—with zero growth, if you invest for m years rather than n, then the amount required to give the same total is n/m times as much each year.

Example 7.2   At the age of 25, you decide to build up savings to fund your retirement. You assume that you'll retire at age 70 and will need a lump sum of one million dollars at that time. You'll pay into your savings fund at the end of each year, you expect the amount that you pay into savings to increase by 2% each year, and you expect that your savings fund will grow at 4% annually.

(a) How much should you plan to save in the first year?

(b) If you were to put off starting to save for 10 years, then what would be the new initial sum?

Solution   Suppose that you have C_n at the beginning of year n, and you start by saving R in the first year. Then

$$C_0 = 0, \text{ and}$$

$$C_{n+1} = C_n \cdot 1.04 + R \cdot 1.02^{n-1},$$

so

$$C_1 = R,$$

$$C_2 = (1.04 + 1.02)R,$$

$$C_3 = (1.04^2 + 1.04 \times 1.02 + 1.02^2)R.$$

Summing geometric series leads to

$$C_n = R\sum_{i=0}^{n-1}1.04^i \times 1.02^{n-1-i}$$

$$= R\frac{1.04^n - 1.02^n}{1.04 - 1.02}$$

$$= 50R(1.04^n - 1.02^n).$$

(a) Saving for 45 years, we want

$$50R(1.04^{45} - 1.02^{45}) = 1,000,000;$$

that is, $R = 20,000/(1.04^{45} - 1.02^{45}) = 5876.61$. You must save about $5,876 in the first year.

(b) Replacing 45 by 35 leads to $R = 10,276.44$. You now must save about $10,276 in the first year—considerably more.

Example 7.3 At the age of 25, Alex decides to save 10% of his income annually. His twin brother Ben will delay starting saving for k years, and then will also save a fixed proportion of his income. Both will retire at age 68. Their incomes are identical and rise by 2% each year. For a growth rate of 4%, what proportion of his income must Ben save to put himself in the same financial position as Alex at retirement age when (a) $k = 5$, (b) $k = 10$.

Solution Let I_j be their income in year j, so

$$I_j = C(1 + x)^j,$$

where $x = 2\%$, and let Y_j be the amount Alex has saved by the end of year j. Suppose that they invest at the beginning of a year and $G = 4\%$ is the growth rate. We have

$$Y_1 = I_1(1 + G)/10$$

and, for $j > 1$,

$$Y_j = (Y_{j-1} + I_j/10) \times (1 + G).$$

This leads to

$$Y_j = \frac{C(1+G)(1+x)}{10}\sum_{r=0}^{j-1}(1+G)^r(1+x)^{j-1-r},$$

which simplifies to

$$\frac{C(1+G)(1+x)}{10} \cdot \frac{(1+G)^j - (1+x)^j}{G-x}.$$

At age 68, Alex will have

$$\frac{C(1+G)(1+x)}{10} \cdot \frac{(1+G)^{43} - (1+x)^{43}}{G-x}.$$

Ben begins to save when his income is $C(1 + x)^{k+1}$. Let Z_j be the amount that Ben has saved by the end of year j, where $j > k$. If he saves proportion p of his income, then

$$Z_{k+1} = I_{k+1}p(1 + G)$$

and

$$Z_{k+r} = (Z_{k+r-1} + pI_{k+r})(1 + G),$$

leading to

$$Z_{k+r} = C(1+G)p(1+x)^{k+1}\frac{(1+G)^r - (1+x)^r}{G-x}.$$

(a) Thus when $k = 5$, at age 68 Ben will have saved

$$C(1+G)p(1+x)^6\frac{(1+G)^{38} - (1+x)^{38}}{G-x};$$

canceling the factor $C(1 + G)$, he will be in Alex's position if

$$\frac{(1+x)}{10} \cdot \frac{(1+G)^{43} - (1+x)^{43}}{G-x} = p(1+x)^6\frac{(1+G)^{38} - (1+x)^{38}}{G-x};$$

that is, if

$$p(1+x)^5 = \frac{(1+G)^{43} - (1+x)^{43}}{10((1+G)^{38} - (1+x)^{38})},$$

then by using the numbers given in the problem we find that $p = 0.1319....$ Ben must save about 13.2% of his income.

(b) When $k = 10$, simply change the 38 to 33 in the expression above. We find that $p = 0.1771...$, so now Ben must save about 17.7% of his income.

8

Student Loans

Repayment terms for student loans vary greatly, so we'll use a framework that you can adapt to your situation. Assume that student loan repayments start a few months after graduation. In each year from then, 9% of the total income of the borrower in excess of some threshold T is paid until the debt is cleared, or 30 years elapse, whichever comes earlier. No payments are required in years when the borrower's income is below T. Interest is charged at the rate of inflation plus an amount that depends on the income that year: this extra amount is zero for incomes below T, is 3% for incomes above some higher level E, and is on a linear sliding scale for incomes between T and E ($T < E$).

Example 8.1 Using the terms given above, create a table that shows how the student loan changes for Joyce, who has an initial loan of $30,000 and a starting salary of $25,000. Let $T = \$21,000$ and $E = \$41,000$. Assume that her salary increases by $2,000 each year, that the inflation rate is 2%, and (for simplicity) that she receives her entire salary at the beginning of the year, but pays the interest due at the year's end.

Solution When Joyce's salary is S, where $21,000 \le S \le 41,000$, the interest rate is

$$(2 + 3(S - 21,000)/20,000)\%.$$

The following table shows a partial repayment schedule. Cash amounts are rounded to the nearest dollar. The last column gives the amount still owed after repaying interest and principal on the outstanding debt. Despite "repaying" $3,600 in total principal ($360 + \cdots + \$1080$),

Joyce owes $1,318 *more* than when she started. Even after five years, her principal repayments still don't exceed the interest charged.

Year	Salary	Interest Rate (%)	Start Loan	Interest Payment	Principal Payment	End Loan
1	25,000	2.60	30,000	780	360	30,420
2	27,000	2.90	30,420	882	540	30,762
3	29,000	3.20	30,762	984	720	31,026
4	31,000	3.50	31,026	1086	900	31,212
5	33,000	3.80	31,212	1186	1080	31,318

Example 8.2 A student graduates with $30,000 in student loan debt. As above, $T = $21,000 and $E = $41,000. Her monthly rent is $800 (including utilities). Income taxes are levied at a flat rate of 32% on all income.

(a) Find the minimum annual salary that she needs to have a monthly income of at least $700 after paying rent, income taxes, and student loan repayments.

(b) If she were paid that salary, then how much of a 10% bonus would she keep?

Solution   (a) She wants to net at least $1,500 ($700 + $800 rent) every month after paying income taxes and student loan repayments; that is, at least $18,000 per year. Given her financial obligations, we can assert that her gross salary must exceed $T = $21,000 (where 9% student loan payments kick in). On a gross salary of exactly $21,000, she loses $21,000 × 0.32 = $6,720 in taxes, so she retains only $14,280. For each dollar over $21,000, she loses $0.32 (taxes) + $0.09 (loan repayments) = $0.41, so to get her extra $18,000 − $14,280 = $3,720 to bring her total to $18,000 she needs another $3,720/(1 − 0.41) = $3,720/0.59 = $6,305.08. Thus her salary must be at least $21,000 + $6,305.08 = $27,305.08.

(b) If she receives a 10% bonus of $2,730.51, then she keeps only 59% of this amount (because it's still subject to income tax and student loan debt), so she keeps $1,611.00.

9 Kelly Strategy

Suppose that you have funds available to invest in a series of speculative ventures. For simplicity, assume that a venture either fails (you lose all money invested) or succeeds (you double the money invested). When is it worth investing and how much should you risk?

Let p be the proportion of times the venture succeeds, and suppose that your criterion is that your funds must increase as fast as possible over the long term. If $p < 0.5$, then on average you'll lose money, so even though this investment strategy might pay off in the short term, in the long run you'll lose.

Now suppose that $p > 0.5$. Even though you succeed more often than you fail, a bold and ambitious approach could easily hit a run of bad luck. If your fortune is F, and you invest it all every time, then on average each investment multiplies your current fortune by $2p$. Because $2p > 1$, on average you achieve exponential growth. After n investments, however, this average is made up of a tiny chance, p^n, of amassing an enormous fortune, and a much larger chance, $1 - p^n$, of losing everything. It's overwhelmingly likely that you'll be completely ruined even though the average outcome is attractive.

On the other hand, if you're cautious and invest only small amounts, then it might take a long time to make a reasonable profit. Suppose that you decide to invest some fraction x of your current fortune, meaning that you will invest more next time after a success, and less after a loss. What value of x is best?

If your fortune is now F, then you invest amount xF. After the venture's outcome, your new fortune is either $(1 - x)F$ after a loss or $(1 + x)F$ after a success. So after each venture, your fortune changes either by the factor $(1 - x)$ or $(1 + x)$, according to the outcome. Consequently, if you begin with X_0 and have S successes and $n - S$ losses in n ventures, then X_n, your new fortune, is

$$X_n = X_0(1 + x)^S(1 - x)^{n-S}.$$

Let $X_n = X_0 \cdot r^n$, where r is the average change in your fortune over each of n investments, so

$$r^n = (1 + x)^S(1 - x)^{n-S}.$$

Take logs and divide by n to get

$$\log(r) = \frac{S}{n}\log(1+x) + \frac{n-S}{n}\log(1-x).$$

When n is large, then S/n, the actual fraction of successful ventures, will be close to p, the long-run proportion of successes, so

$$\log(r) \approx p \log(1 + x) + (1 - p) \log(1 - x).$$

We want to find the value of x that makes the growth rate r as large as possible, so let

$$f(x) = p \log(1 + x) + (1 - p) \log(1 - x)$$

and differentiate to get

$$f'(x) = \frac{p}{1+x} - \frac{1-p}{1-x}.$$

Set the right side equal to zero for a maximum, yielding

$$p(1 - x) = (1 - p)(1 + x),$$

so the solution is $x = 2p - 1$.

And because

$$f''(x) = \frac{-p}{(1+x)^2} - \frac{1-p}{(1-x)^2} < 0,$$

this solution is indeed a maximum. We now have the **Kelly strategy,** named after John L. Kelly, who derived it in 1956. We conclude that the growth rate is maximized if we invest the fraction $2p - 1$ of our fortune.

Because

$$f(2p-1) = p\log(2p) + (1-p)\log(2-2p)$$
$$= \log(2p^p(1-p)^{1-p}),$$

the optimum growth rate is

$$r = 2p^p(1-p)^{1-p}.$$

The Kelly strategy is also called the Kelly criterion, Kelly formula, or Kelly bet.

Example 9.1 If $p = 0.55$, then $2p - 1 = 0.1$ and we should invest 10% of our current fortune. The long-term growth rate of our wealth is $r = 2 \times 0.55^{0.55} \times 0.45^{0.45} = 1.00502$ each time; that is, about half of one percent. Disappointing as this sounds, it's the best you can do when $p = 0.55$. The graph of $f(x)$ when $p = 0.55$ is shown in the following figure.

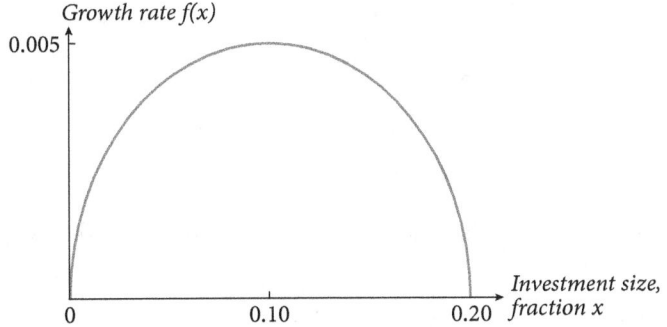

If $x > 0.2$, then the growth rate is negative even though the odds are in your favor for each individual investment. So if you greedily risk 25% of your wealth on investments with a 55% chance of doubling up and a 45% chance of total loss, then the arithmetic shows that, in the long run, you'll lose about two-thirds of one percent of your wealth each time.

The next two examples apply these ideas to the context of betting on the spins of a roulette wheel, rather than investing in speculative business ventures—the mathematics is identical.

Example 9.2   Suppose that a roulette wheel in a casino is so biased that it shows red numbers 60% of the time. A winning bet on red doubles your money.

(a) Find the Kelly strategy that maximizes the long-term growth of your fortune.

(b) Use the Rule of 72 to estimate how many bets it will take you to double your money.

(c) What is the smallest value of x such that if you bet x% of your fortune each time, then you're certain to be ruined?

Solution   (a) $p = 0.6$ so the Kelly strategy is to bet 20% of your current fortune each time. Thus the mean growth rate per bet is $r = 2 \times 0.6^{0.6} \times 0.4^{0.4} = 1.02033\ldots$; that is, about 2% per bet.

(b) By the Rule of 72, it will take about $72/2 = 36$ bets to double your fortune.

(c) To find the critical point where betting too much leads to ruin, solve

$$0.6 \log(1 + x) + 0.4 \log(1 - x) = 0;$$

that is,

$$(1 + x)^{0.6} \times (1 - x)^{0.4} = 1.$$

To solve this equation, raise both sides to the fifth power, and rewrite it as

$$(1 - x)^2 = (1 + x)^{-3},$$

giving the iteration

$$x_{n+1} = 1 - (1 + x_n)^{-3/2},$$

which converges to $x = 0.38939\ldots$. If you bet more than 39% of your fortune regularly, then you'll lose it all in the long run.

Example 9.3   Suppose that the chance a roulette wheel shows red is $p = 0.75$, and winning bets are paid at even money. Describe the strategy that maximizes the rate at which you expect your fortune to increase. Under this strategy, use the Rule of 72 to estimate how many bets it takes you to double your money.

Solution We know that the optimum strategy is to bet the fraction $2p - 1$ of your current fortune, giving an estimated growth rate of

$$r = 2p^p(1-p)^{1-p}.$$

Thus, when $p = 0.75$, you should bet 50% of your current fortune each time. The estimated growth rate $r = 2 \times 0.75^{0.75} \times 0.25^{0.25} = 1.1397...$, or just under 14%, so by the Rule of 72 it will take 5 or 6 bets to double your money.

Example 9.4 Suppose that, as described earlier, you will invest a fixed fraction of your current capital in a series of speculative ventures. If a venture fails, then you lose the whole amount invested, but if it succeeds, then you get your investment back, plus a profit of α times the amount invested. Let p denote the proportion of such investments that succeed, with $p > 1/(1 + \alpha)$ so that, on average, you make a profit.

(a) Generalize the original argument to this case, showing that your capital is expected to increase fastest when $x = (p(1 + \alpha) - 1)/\alpha$, and find the corresponding rate at which your capital increases.

(b) If $p = 20\%$ and $\alpha = 5$, then estimate how many investments it will take for your initial capital to double.

Solution (a) When your capital is F, you invest xF, so you have $(1 - x)F$ left if the venture fails or $F + \alpha xF$ if it succeeds. After n investments that include w wins and $n - w$ losses, your fortune will be

$$F(1 + x\alpha)^w(1 - x)^{n-w},$$

which in the long run we expect to be of the form Fr^n, where r is the growth rate. Thus

$$r^n = (1 + x\alpha)^w(1 - x)^{n-w}.$$

Take logs and divide by n. We expect w/n to be close to p, so

$$\log(r) \approx p \log(1 + x\alpha) + (1 - p) \log(1 - x) = f(x).$$

Then

$$f'(x) = \frac{p\alpha}{1 + x\alpha} - \frac{1-p}{1-x}.$$

Equate this to zero (a maximum) and solve for x to get

$$x = (p(1 + \alpha) - 1)/\alpha,$$

which checks when $\alpha = 1$, because this answer collapses to $2p - 1$ as required.

The growth rate r comes from

$$\log(r) \approx p \log(1 + p(1 + \alpha) - 1) + (1 - p) \log((1 - p)(1 + \alpha)/\alpha),$$

so

$$\log(r) \approx \log(p^p \cdot (1 - p)^{1-p} \cdot (1 + \alpha)/\alpha^{1-p});$$

that is,

$$r \approx (1 + \alpha)p^p \cdot (1 - p)^{1-p}/\alpha^{1-p}.$$

(b) If $p = 20\%$ and $\alpha = 5$, then the optimal proportion to invest is

$$x = (0.2 \times 6 - 1)/5 = 4\%,$$

which leads to an approximate growth rate of

$$r = 6 \times 0.2^{0.2} \times 0.8^{0.8}/5^{0.8} = 1.0038\ldots,$$

or about 0.38%. By the Rule of 72, about $72/0.38 \approx 190$ investments (bets) are needed to double your fortune.

10   Mathematics Review

Key Facts

- Constants

  $e = 2.71828182\ldots,$

  $\log(2) = \log_e(2) = \ln(2) = 0.69314718\ldots,$

  $\log(1) = 0,$

  $\log(\frac{1}{2}) = -\log(2) = -0.69314718\ldots.$

- Sums

  $$\sum_{i=1}^{n} i = 1 + 2 + 3 + \cdots + n = \frac{n(n+1)}{2},$$

  $$\sum_{i=1}^{n} i^2 = 1^2 + 2^2 + 3^2 + \cdots + n^2 = \frac{n(n+1)(2n+1)}{6}.$$

- Taylor series expansions

  $$\frac{1}{1-x} = \sum_{n=0}^{\infty} x^n = 1 + x + x^2 + x^3 + \cdots, \quad \text{for } |x| < 1;$$

  $$\frac{1}{1+x} = \sum_{n=0}^{\infty} (-1)^n x^n = 1 - x + x^2 - x^3 + \cdots, \quad \text{for } |x| < 1;$$

  $$\log(1-x) = -\sum_{n=1}^{\infty} \frac{x^n}{n} = -x - \frac{x^2}{2} - \frac{x^3}{3} - \frac{x^4}{4} - \cdots, \quad \text{for } |x| < 1;$$

$$\log(1+x) = \sum_{n=1}^{\infty} (-1)^{n+1} \frac{x^n}{n} = x - \frac{x^2}{2} + \frac{x^3}{3} - \frac{x^4}{4} + \cdots, \quad \text{for } |x| < 1;$$

$$e^x = \sum_{n=0}^{\infty} \frac{x^n}{n!} = 1 + x + \frac{x^2}{2!} + \frac{x^3}{3!} + \cdots, \quad \text{for all } x.$$

- For $x \neq 1$, the sum of the first n terms of a geometric series is

$$a + ax + ax^2 + ax^3 + \cdots + ax^{n-1} = \sum_{k=0}^{n-1} ax^k = a \left(\frac{1-x^n}{1-x} \right),$$

where a is the first term of the series and x is the common ratio. When $a = 1$, this equality simplifies to

$$1 + x + x^2 + x^3 + \cdots + x^{n-1} = \frac{1-x^n}{1-x} = \frac{x^n - 1}{x - 1}.$$

- As $n \to \infty$, the absolute value of x must be less than one for the geometric series to converge. The sum then becomes

$$a + ax + ax^2 + ax^3 + \cdots = \sum_{k=0}^{\infty} ax^k = \frac{a}{1-x}, \quad \text{for } |x| < 1.$$

When $a = 1$, this equality simplifies to

$$1 + x + x^2 + x^3 + \cdots = \frac{1}{1-x}.$$

- For fixed x,

$$\lim_{n \to \infty} \left(1 + \frac{x}{n} \right)^n = e^x = \exp(x).$$

Integer Exponents

In general, an is defined by $a^n = a \cdot a \cdots a$ (n factors) for any positive integer n. For example, $a^2 = a \cdot a$, $a^3 = a \cdot a \cdot a$, and $a^4 = a \cdot a \cdot a \cdot a$. The rules of exponents are:

Rule	Example
$a^m a^n = a^{m+n}$	$a^2 a^3 = \underbrace{(a \cdot a)}_{2}\underbrace{(a \cdot a \cdot a)}_{3} = \underbrace{a \cdot a \cdot a \cdot a \cdot a}_{5 \text{ factors}} = a^5$
$\dfrac{a^m}{a^n} = a^{m-n}$	$\dfrac{a^5}{a^3} = \dfrac{a \cdot a \cdot a \cdot a \cdot a}{a \cdot a \cdot a} = \dfrac{a \cdot a \cdot a}{a \cdot a \cdot a} \cdot \dfrac{a \cdot a}{1} = a \cdot a = a^2$
$(a^m)^n = a^{mn}$	$(a^3)^2 = (a \cdot a \cdot a)(a \cdot a \cdot a) = a \cdot a \cdot a \cdot a \cdot a \cdot a = a^6$
$(ab)^n = a^n b^n$	$(ab)^3 = (a \cdot b)(a \cdot b)(a \cdot b) = a \cdot a \cdot a \cdot b \cdot b \cdot b = a^3 b^3$
$\left(\dfrac{a}{b}\right)^n = \dfrac{a^n}{b^n}$	$\left(\dfrac{a}{b}\right)^4 = \left(\dfrac{a}{b}\right)\left(\dfrac{a}{b}\right)\left(\dfrac{a}{b}\right)\left(\dfrac{a}{b}\right) = \dfrac{a \cdot a \cdot a \cdot a}{b \cdot b \cdot b \cdot b} = \dfrac{a^4}{b^4}$

If $a \neq 0$, then the rule $a^m a^n = a^{m+n}$ suggests a logical way to define a^0. Because we want the equation $a^0 a^n = a^{0+n} = a^n$ to be true, a^0 should leave an unchanged by multiplication. Therefore, a^0 is defined by

$$a^0 = 1$$

Similarly, for the equation $a^n a^{-n} = a^{n-n} = a^0 = 1$ to hold, a^{-n} must be the reciprocal of a^n. Therefore, a^{-n} is defined by

$$a^{-n} = \frac{1}{a^n}.$$

With these two definitions, the rules of exponents hold for all integer exponents, positive, negative, or zero.

You can move any factor a^n from the numerator to the denominator or vice versa by changing the sign of the exponent. The following examples show how to rewrite expressions to have all positive exponents.

$$a^5 b^{-6} = a^5 \cdot \frac{1}{b^6} = \frac{a^5}{b^6}, \qquad \frac{1}{a^{-4}} = \frac{1}{\dfrac{1}{a^4}} = a^4, \qquad \frac{a^{-2}}{b^3} = \frac{\dfrac{1}{a^2}}{b^3} = \frac{1}{a^2 b^3}.$$

Rational Exponents

Here we define exponentiation by rational numbers in such a way that the rules for integer exponents remain valid. Rational numbers take the form m/n, where m and n are integers and $n \neq 0$.

Because we want the equation $(a^{1/2})^2 = a^{(1/2) \cdot 2} = a^1 = a$ to be true, $a^{1/2}$ is defined as

$$a^{1/2} = \sqrt{a}.$$

Similarly,

$$a^{1/3} = \sqrt[3]{a}.$$

In general,

$$a^{1/n} = \sqrt[n]{a}$$

for any positive integer n. For example,

$$9^{1/2} = \sqrt{9} = 3, \qquad\qquad 64^{1/3} = \sqrt[3]{64} = 4,$$

$$(-27)^{1/3} = \sqrt[3]{-27} = -3, \qquad 16^{1/4} = \sqrt[4]{16} = 2.$$

Now that the expression $a^{1/n}$ makes sense, we can generalize to $a^{m/n}$, where m/n is a rational number. Assume that any fraction used as an exponent is written in **lowest terms**; that is, in the form m/n where n is a positive integer, m is an integer (positive, negative, or zero), and m and n have no common factors greater than 1. We want $(a^{m/n})^n = a^m$ to hold, so that $a^{m/n}$ is the nth root of a^m. Therefore, $a^{m/n}$ is defined as

$$a^{m/n} = \sqrt[n]{a^m}.$$

For example,

$$4^{3/2} = \sqrt{4^3} = \sqrt{64} = 8,$$

$$8^{2/3} = \sqrt[3]{8^2} = \sqrt[3]{64} = 4,$$

$$a^{2/7} \cdot a^{5/2} = a^{4/14} \cdot a^{35/14} = a^{39/14} = \sqrt[14]{a^{39}},$$

$$\frac{a^{2/3}}{a^{3/5}} = a^{(2/3-3/5)} = a^{1/15} = \sqrt[15]{a},$$

$$\frac{\sqrt[3]{a^4}}{\sqrt[4]{a^3}} = \frac{a^{4/3}}{a^{3/4}} = a^{(4/3-3/4)} = a^{7/12} = \sqrt[12]{a^7}.$$

It's sometimes handy to use the fact $a^{m/n} = \sqrt[n]{a^m} = (\sqrt[n]{a})^m$ in calculations. For example, $8^{2/3}$ is easy to evaluate either as

$$8^{2/3} = \sqrt[3]{8^2} = \sqrt[3]{64} = 4$$

or as

$$8^{2/3} = (\sqrt[3]{8})^2 = 2^2 = 4.$$

However, $32^{3/5}$ is hard to evaluate as

$$32^{3/5} = \sqrt[5]{32^3}$$

but easy to evaluate as

$$32^{3/5} = (\sqrt[5]{32})^3 = 2^3 = 8.$$

Logarithms

Logarithms are exponents. In the equation $100 = 10^2$, for example, the exponent 2 is the logarithm of 100 to the base 10. To understand logarithms, first note that the equations

$$x = 2y \quad \text{and} \quad y = \tfrac{1}{2}x$$

are in fact only one equation that expresses the same relation between x and y, written first in a form solved for x and second in a form solved for y. Similarly, if a is any constant > 1, then the equations

$$x = a^y \quad \text{and} \quad y = \log_a x$$

are equivalent, except that the second equation is solved for y and the symbol "$\log_a$" denotes this operation. The following examples show equivalent statements about exponents (on the left) and logarithms (on the right).

$$1000 = 10^3, \qquad 3 = \log_{10} 100,$$

$$16 = 2^4, \qquad 4 = \log_2 16,$$

$$2 = 8^{1/3}, \qquad \frac{1}{3} = \log_8 2,$$

$$\frac{1}{9} = 3^{-2}, \qquad -2 = \log_3 \frac{1}{9},$$

$$1 = a^0, \qquad 0 = \log_a 1.$$

The rules for logarithms are derived from the corresponding rules for exponents:

Rule	Proof
$\log_a x_1 x_2 = \log_a x_1 + \log_a x_2$	$x_1 x_2 = a^{y_1} \cdot a^{y_2} = a^{y_1 + y_2}$
$\log_a \dfrac{x_1}{x_2} = \log_a x_1 - \log_a x_2$	$\dfrac{x_1}{x_2} = \dfrac{a^{y_1}}{a^{y_2}} = a^{y_1 - y_2}$
$\log_a x^n = n \log_a x$	$x^n = (a^y)^n = a^{ny}$

To prove the first rule in detail, note that if

$$x_1 = a^{y_1} \quad \text{and} \quad x_2 = a^{y_2},$$

or equivalently,

$$y_1 = \log_a x_1 \quad \text{and} \quad y_2 = \log_a x_2,$$

then by the rule of exponents,

$$x_1 x_2 = a^{y_1} \cdot a^{y_2} = a^{y_1 + y_2}.$$

The exponent on the right, which is $\log_a x_1 x_2$, is also $\log_a x_1 + \log_a x_2$, and this is the first rule. The other two rules are proved similarly.

Two more useful facts about logarithms are

$$a^{\log_a x} = x \quad \text{and} \quad \log_a a^x = x.$$

The first fact means that when x is expressed as some power of a, the exponent *is* $\log_a x$. The second fact means that the left side *is* the exponent when a^x is expressed as some power of a.

If you need to shift logarithms from one base to another, note that

$$x = b^y = \left(a^{\log_a b} \right)^y = a^{y \log_a b}$$

which translates to

$$\log_a x = (\log_a b)(\log_b x).$$

In most applications, logarithms to the base e or base 2 are used. Base 10 rarely appears in numerical calculations.

Geometric Progressions & Series

A **geometric progression** is a sequence of numbers in which each term after the first is obtained from the one that precedes it by multiplying by a fixed number called the **ratio**:

$$a, ar, ar^2, ar^3, \ldots, ar^n, \ldots \qquad (r = \text{the ratio})$$

For example,

2,	4,	8,	16,	...,	$r = 2$
2,	6,	18,	54,	...,	$r = 3$
1,	$\dfrac{1}{2}$,	$\dfrac{1}{4}$,	$\dfrac{1}{8}$,	...,	$r = \dfrac{1}{2}$
2	$-\dfrac{2}{3}$,	$\dfrac{2}{9}$,	$-\dfrac{2}{27}$,	...,	$r = -\dfrac{1}{3}$

The sum S of the first n terms of a geometric progression is

$$S = a + ar + ar^2 + ar^3 + \cdots + ar^n$$

or

$$S = \frac{a(1 - r^{n+1})}{1 - r}.$$

To prove that these two formulas are equivalent (assuming $r \neq 1$, because $r = 1$ makes the second formula meaningless), multiply the first formula through by r to get

$$Sr = ar + ar^2 + ar^3 + \cdots + ar^{n+1}$$

and then subtract this result from the first formula, cancelling all the common terms:

$$S = a + ar + ar^2 + \cdots + ar^n$$
$$Sr = ar + ar^2 + ar^3 + \cdots + ar^{n+1}$$

From these cancellations, it's clear that

$$S - Sr = a - ar^{n+1},$$

or

$$S(1-r) = a(1-r^{n+1}),$$

which is equivalent to

$$S = \frac{a(1-r^{n+1})}{1-r}.$$

To extend the sum S to an infinite number of terms, use dots in the following way

$$a + ar + ar^2 + ar^3 + \cdots + ar^n + \cdots$$

This sum is called a **geometric series**. Its value—if it has one—is determined by examining the behavior of the **partial sum**

$$S = a + ar + ar^2 + ar^3 + \cdots + ar^n$$

as the positive integer n increases. By using the formula for S given above, this partial sum can be written in the form

$$S = \frac{a(1-r^{n+1})}{1-r} = \frac{a}{1-r} - \frac{a}{1-r}r^{n+1}.$$

If the ratio r is any number numerically less than 1, that is, if $|r| < 1$, then the second term on the right,

$$\frac{a}{1-r}r^{n+1},$$

approaches zero as n increases. (As a number numerically less than one is raised to higher and higher powers, it gets smaller and smaller.)

This concept is expressed as

$$\frac{a}{1-r}r^{n+1} \to 0 \quad \text{as } n \to \infty,$$

where the arrow means "approaches." For these values of r we therefore have

$$S = a + ar + ar^2 + \cdots + ar^n \to \frac{a}{1-r} \quad \text{as } n \to \infty,$$

which is what is meant by the statement that the formula

$$a + ar + ar^2 + \cdots + ar^n + \cdots = \frac{a}{1-r}$$

is valid for $|r| < 1$.

The formula for $a/(1-r)$ can be used to show that any infinite repeating decimal represents a rational number. For example, to see why

$$0.3333\ldots = \frac{1}{3}$$

is true, use the meaning of the decimal and apply the $a/(1-r)$ formula:

$$0.3333\ldots = \frac{3}{10} + \frac{3}{10^2} + \frac{3}{10^3} + \cdots$$

$$= \frac{3}{10} + \left(\frac{3}{10}\right)\left(\frac{1}{10}\right) + \left(\frac{3}{10}\right)\left(\frac{1}{10}\right)^2 + \cdots$$

$$= \frac{\dfrac{3}{10}}{1 - \dfrac{1}{10}} = \frac{3}{10} \cdot \frac{10}{9} = \frac{1}{3}.$$

Arithmetic Progressions

An **arithmetic progression** is a sequence of numbers in which each term after the first is obtained from the one that precedes it by adding a fixed number called the **common difference**:

$$a, a + d, a + 2d, \ldots, a + (n-1)d.$$

The simplest and most important arithmetic progression is the first n positive integers:

$$1, 2, 3, \ldots, n.$$

If S denotes the sum of this progression,

$$S = 1 + 2 + 3 + \cdots + n,$$

then a formula for S has many uses. To find this formula, write the sum twice, once as given and the second time in reverse order:

$$S = 1 + 2 + 3 + \cdots + n$$
$$S = n + (n-1) + (n-2) + \cdots + 1$$

Adding the two expressions yields $2S$ on the left; and because each column on the right adds up to $n + 1$ and there are n columns, we get

$$2S = n(n + 1),$$

or

$$S = \frac{n(n+1)}{2}.$$

Sigma Notation

Mathematicians use a concise way of writing the sum of a list of $n + 1$ terms like $a_m, a_{m+1}, a_{m+2}, \ldots, a_{m+n}$, where m and n are integers and $n \geq 0$. This notation is called **sigma notation** because it involves the capital Greek letter Σ (sigma, for *sum*); we use it to represent a summation by writing

$$a_m + a_{m+1} + a_{m+2} + \cdots + a_{m+n} = \sum_{i=m}^{m+n} a_i.$$

Here, the letter i is called the **index** of the summation, and this index spans all integers starting with the **lower limit** m and continuing up to and including the **upper limit** $m + n$.

We can use sigma notation as shown in the following examples.

$$\sum_{i=3}^{7} a_i = a_3 + a_4 + a_5 + a_6 + a_7 = \sum_{j=3}^{7} a_j.$$

The preceding example shows that there's nothing special about the letter i.

$$\sum_{i=1}^{4} i^2 = 1^2 + 2^2 + 3^2 + 4^2 = 30 = \sum_{k=0}^{4} k^2, \text{ because } 0^2 = 0.$$

$$\sum_{i=11}^{100} i^3 = 11^3 + 12^3 + 13^3 + \cdots + 100^3$$

$$= \sum_{j=12}^{101} (j-1)^3 = \sum_{k=10}^{99} (k+1)^3.$$

$$\sum_{i=7}^{10} 2i = 2(7) + 2(8) + 2(9) + 2(10) = 68$$

$$= 2(34) = 2(7 + 8 + 9 + 10)$$

$$= 2\sum_{i=7}^{10} i.$$

$$\sum_{i=3}^{3} a_i = a_3 = \sum_{i=4}^{4} a_{i-1} = \sum_{i=2}^{2} a_{i+1}.$$

$$\sum_{i=1}^{5} a = a + a + a + a + a = 5a.$$

Means

The most common type of mean is the **arithmetic mean** (often simply called the mean or the average). The arithmetic mean of the n numbers $x_1, x_2, \ldots, x_n$ is the sum of the x_i's divided by n, or

$$AM = \frac{1}{n}\sum_{i=1}^{n} x_i = \frac{1}{n}(x_1 + x_2 + \cdots + x_n).$$

The **geometric mean** of n positive numbers is the nth root of the product of all n numbers. In other words, the geometric mean is the antilog of the arithmetic mean of the logs of the numbers $x_1, x_2, \ldots, x_n$ (all $x_i > 0$), or

$$GM = \sqrt[n]{\prod_{i=1}^{n} x_i} = \sqrt[n]{x_1 x_2 \cdots x_n}.$$

The **harmonic mean** of the numbers $x_1, x_2, \ldots, x_n$ (all $x_i \neq 0$) is the reciprocal of the arithmetic mean of the reciprocals of the x_i's:

$$HM = \frac{1}{\dfrac{1}{n}\sum_{i=1}^{n}\dfrac{1}{x_i}} = \frac{n}{\dfrac{1}{x_1} + \dfrac{1}{x_2} + \cdots + \dfrac{1}{x_n}}.$$

The inequality $AM \geq GM \geq HM$ holds for any set of positive numbers.

Factorials

Factorial notation lets us represent the product of consecutive positive integers concisely. For an integer $n \geq 0$, n **factorial** (denoted by $n!$) is defined by

$$0! = 1,$$
$$n! = (n)(n-1)(n-2)\cdots(3)(2)(1), \qquad \text{for } n \geq 1.$$

So $0! = 1! = 1$, $2! = 2$, $3! = 6$, $4! = 24$, and $5! = 120$. Also, for every $n \geq 0$, $(n+1)! = (n+1)(n!)$.

Note that $n!$ grows rapidly. $10! = 3{,}628{,}800$ is exactly the number of seconds in six weeks, $11!$ exceeds the number of seconds in one year, $12!$ exceeds the number in 12 years, and $13!$ surpasses the number of seconds in a century.

Taylor Series

A **Taylor series** represents a function as an infinite sum of terms that are calculated from the values of the function's derivatives at a single point a. The function $f(x)$ must be infinitely differentiable at a (or, for approximations, differentiable as often as we need). The Taylor series (or Taylor expansion) of $f(x)$ about the point a is

$$f(a) + (x-a)\frac{f'(a)}{1!} + (x-a)^2 \frac{f''(a)}{2!} + (x-a)^3 \frac{f'''(a)}{3!} + \cdots,$$

which can be written more compactly by using sigma notation as

$$\sum_{n=0}^{\infty}(x-a)^n \frac{f^{(n)}(a)}{n!},$$

where $n!$ denotes the factorial of n and $f^{(n)}(a)$ denotes the nth derivative of f evaluated at the point a. The derivative of order zero of f is defined to be f itself and $(x-a)^0 = 1$ and $0! = 1$.

A Taylor series centered at zero is known as a **Maclaurin series**:

$$f(0) + xf'(0) + x^2 \frac{f''(0)}{2!} + x^3 \frac{f'''(0)}{3!} + \cdots.$$

Provided that these series converge, the first few terms can be expected to approximate f well for values near a, or near zero, respectively.

L'Hôpital's Rule

Let a be a real number and let $f(x)$ and $g(x)$ be functions that are differentiable on some open interval containing a. Assume also that $g'(x) \neq 0$ on this interval, except possibly at the point a itself. If $f(a) = 0$ and $g(a) = 0$, then

$$\lim_{x \to a} \frac{f(x)}{g(x)} = \lim_{x \to a} \frac{f'(x)}{g'(x)},$$

provided that the limit on the right exists.

Iteration

To solve $f(x) = 0$ by using **Newton-Raphson iteration**, make an initial guess $x_0 = c$, and then calculate $x_1, x_2, \ldots$ from the iteration $x_{n+1} = x_n - f(x_n)/f'(x_n)$, where f' is the derivative of f. If the sequence converges to a limit, then that limit is a solution.

To solve $f(x) = 0$ by using **fixed-point iteration**, convert $f(x) = 0$ algebraically to the form $x = g(x)$, make an initial guess $x_0 = c$, and then calculate $x_1, x_2, \ldots$ from the iteration $x_{n+1} = g(x_n)$. If x_0 is close enough to the solution and $|g'(x)| < 1$ for x near the desired root, then the sequence will converge to a solution as required.

Index